Mama Says . . .
Cookies Cure
a Lot of Things

Visit Tyndale's exciting Web site at www.tyndale.com

Edited by Lisa A. Jackson

Designed by Beth Sparkman

ISBN 0-8423-5192-2

Printed in China

06	05	04	03	02
5	4	3	2	1

Cookies Cure
a Lot of Things

Rita J. Maggart

TYNDALE

Tyndale House Publishers, Inc.
Wheaton, Illinois

*Dedicated to
Mother and Memama*

Acknowledgments

The gestation of *Mama Says* began with a casual conversation with an acquaintance at my church about my need for help with the promotion of my first book, *In the Growing Places*. She suggested that I call Amy Lyles Wilson, then an editor with a publishing house in Nashville. Amy and I met and she sent me to Sabrina Cashwell, a book publicist. Sabrina led me to Evergreen Ideas and the book and product development team of Andy Hyde and Debbie Bush. Andy and Debbie presented my ideas to many publishers. We were excited when Tyndale House Publishers came to Nashville and gave us an interview. Andy and Debbie believed in my ability, and Tyndale House saw the potential of *Mama Says* as a way to communicate with Christian parents.

After contract negotiations with my attorney, Derek Crownover, and with my agreement in hand, I could then return to Amy Lyles Wilson and say, "Let's get to work!" With her guidance and the expert computer skills of Mary MacKinnon, the manuscript began to develop. The give-and-take of Tyndale House editors Karen Watson and Lisa Jackson and art director Beth Sparkman, along with the skill of artist Luke Daab, proved to be a blending of talented business professionals to develop a quality book.

These people have given this book life outside of my home. But *Mama Says* was conceived inside my home as I searched for better ways to communicate with my children. Thanks to my husband, John, and our three sons, Brad, Bill, and Stephen, I was given a reason to grow and mature as a wife and mother. My mother, grandmothers, and mother-in-law knew it would take all the mothers I could get to raise these three boys to manhood, and so we nurtured them together.

The birthing of this book has taken business professionals, friends, and family members, and it hasn't happened overnight. The fine art of mothering doesn't happen overnight either. For me, it began with the birth of my first child in 1974 and will continue for the rest of my life. Sharing what's inside my heart is my job, and remember, it's your job, too.

Rita J. Maggart

*Throughout this book
you'll see the symbol · O · .
This is a secret we use in our family
to send the message* I Love You.

Dear friends,

Hopes and dreams, fears and anxieties, joys and blessings, wor-
ries and concerns—all these emotions and more are wrapped
up in the experience of parenting. Your child-rearing years will
be some of the most exhilarating days of your life, and that's as
it should be. Only days into your child's life, he or she will begin
to test you. The main question you'll probably be asking yourself is, "How do I prepare myself for raising this child?" There is
an answer. God is so good, he has given us many books of
instruction on parenting—together they're called the Bible. All
too often, the media and other children have more of an influence on our children's values than we do. There is something
we can do, however, something that's active rather than pas-
sive. We must apply the same energy and thoughtfulness to
raising our children that we apply to pursuing our careers. It's
never too early or too late to start thinking about what you
want to communicate to your child. And the best way to be
prepared for this communication is to write down what you
want to remember. The key to this kind of writing is not found
in the writing itself, but in listening. Listening is learning, and

learning comes from reading, studying, and pondering about what God wants you to say to your child. With that in mind, you can feel confident that what you need to say is not from yourself but from God.

As you begin to build your repertoire of words, you will also begin to refine your thoughts. Your best resource is the Bible. Let your children see it as your best friend and companion. Armed with God's Word, you will be ready to "tell your children what they need to hear, and that's the best you can do"—as my own mama says.

And remember, we're all in this together.

Your friend,
Rita J. Maggart

Mama Says...

Children are a gift from God.

· O ·

I asked the LORD to give me this child, and he has given
me my request. Now I am giving him to the LORD,
and he will belong to the LORD his whole life.
1 SAMUEL 1:27-28

Catch your children being good.

· O ·

Encourage each other and build each other up,
just as you are already doing.
1 THESSALONIANS 5:11

Wake up grateful for what you have rather than grumpy about what you don't have.

· O ·

It is good to give thanks to the LORD, to sing praises to the Most High. It is good to proclaim your unfailing love in the morning.

PSALM 92:1-2

Cookies cure a lot of things.

· O ·

My child, eat honey, for it is good,
and the honeycomb is sweet to the taste.
PROVERBS 24:13

Mama Says...

Coming home for comfort food
is more than mere nourishment.

· O ·

Have something to eat before you go.
JUDGES 19:5

Enjoy your children.

· O ·

Esau looked at the women and children and asked,
"Who are these people with you?" "These are the children
God has graciously given to me," Jacob replied.
GENESIS 33:5

Mama Says...

Learn from your children how to love God.

· O ·

Out of the mouth of babes and sucklings
thou hast perfected praise.
MATTHEW 21:16, KJV

The best gift
you can give your child
is to love his daddy.

· O ·

Didn't the LORD make you one with your wife? In body and
spirit you are his. And what does he want? Godly children
from your union. So guard yourself; remain loyal to the wife
of your youth. "For I hate divorce!" says the LORD.

MALACHI 2:15-16

Mama Says...

Teach your child how to live *and* how to die.

· O ·

A good reputation is more valuable than the most
expensive perfume. In the same way, the day you
die is better than the day you are born.

ECCLESIASTES 7:1

Protect your child's childhood.
She can only be a child once.

· O ·

There is a time for everything, a season
for every activity under heaven.
ECCLESIASTES 3:1

Bedtime is a great time to tell your
child why he's so special.

· O ·

Children are a gift from the LORD;
they are a reward from him.
PSALM 127:3

Make room in your family for people who make mistakes.

· O ·

Stop judging others, and you will not be judged.
Stop criticizing others, or it will all come back on you.
If you forgive others, you will be forgiven.

LUKE 6:37

Mama Says...

Food and conversation go together.
Get to know your child over
a peanut butter sandwich.

· O ·

Let your conversation be gracious and effective
so that you will have the right answer for everyone.
COLOSSIANS 4:6

Let your face glow and not glare.

· O ·

Wisdom lights up a person's face, softening its hardness.
ECCLESIASTES 8:1

Mama Says...

Grow *with* your child, not apart from her.

· O ·

Rejoice. Change your ways. Encourage each other.
Live in harmony and peace. Then the God of
love and peace will be with you.

2 CORINTHIANS 13:11

I can't carry you forever in my arms, but I can carry you forever in my heart.

· O ·

Mary treasured all these things, pondering them in her heart.

LUKE 2:19, NASB

Hug your child—it works miracles.

· O ·

As many as touched were made perfectly whole.

MATTHEW 14:36, KJV

We just *think* babies don't come
with an instruction book.

· O ·

Your word is a lamp for my feet and a light for my path.
PSALM 119:105

Mama Says. . .

Life's not fair.

· O ·

I have observed something else in this world of ours.
The fastest runner doesn't always win the race,
and the strongest warrior doesn't always win the battle.
The wise are often poor, and the skillful are not necessarily
wealthy. And those who are educated don't always lead
successful lives. It is all decided by chance,
by being at the right place at the right time.

ECCLESIASTES 9:11

A thousand times a day, in a
thousand kinds of ways your child
is asking, "Do you love me?"

· O ·

Perfect love expels all fear.
1 JOHN 4:18

What good is it if you love a child
only when he pleases you?

· O ·

If you love only those who love you, what good is that?
MATTHEW 5:46

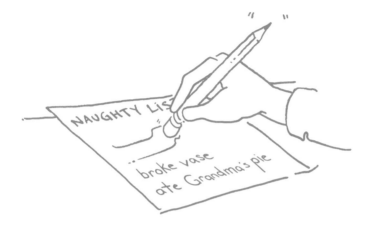

Love is the big eraser.

· O ·

Most important of all, continue to show deep love for
each other, for love covers a multitude of sins.

1 PETER 4:8

Mama Says...

Love unconditionally.

· O ·

Love is patient and kind. Love is not jealous or boastful
or proud or rude. Love does not demand its own way.
Love is not irritable, and it keeps no record of when
it has been wronged. It is never glad about injustice
but rejoices whenever the truth wins out. Love never
gives up, never loses faith, is always hopeful,
and endures through every circumstance.
1 CORINTHIANS 13:4-7

Marriage is a
covenant and
children are a bond.

· O ·

Since they are no longer two but one, let no one
separate them, for God has joined them together.

MATTHEW 19:6

Stop and smell the flowers with your child.

· O ·

Stop and consider the wonderful miracles of God!

JOB 37:14

How do you teach your child to conquer a huge task? The same way you conquer a huge task—little by little.

· O ·

Order on order, order on order,
Line on line, line on line,
A little here, a little there.
ISAIAH 28:10, NASB

Keep your promises.

· O ·

He always remembers his covenant.

PSALM 111:5

It's okay to drop everything and
read to your child.

· O ·

If you wait for perfect conditions,
you will never get anything done.
ECCLESIASTES 11:4

Mama Says...

Every day I will say,
"Something wonderful
is on the way!"

· O ·

When Elizabeth heard Mary's greeting, the baby leaped in
her womb; and Elizabeth was filled with the Holy Spirit.

LUKE 1:41, NASB

Taking care of people is more
important than taking care of things.

· O ·

"Comfort, comfort my people," says your God.
ISAIAH 40:1

The child who is the hardest to love is the
one who needs love the most.

· O ·

Filled with love and compassion, he ran to his son,
embraced him, and kissed him.
LUKE 15:20

A right relationship with God is the beginning
of a right relationship with your child.

· O ·

With God all things are possible.
MATTHEW 19:26, KJV

Mama Says...

Give yourself a
"time-out."

· O ·

He lets me rest in green meadows; he leads me beside
peaceful streams. He renews my strength.

PSALM 23:2-3

Would you want someone to answer *your*
question with, "Because I said so"?

· O ·

A gentle answer turns away wrath,
but harsh words stir up anger.
PROVERBS 15:1

Hold up your shoulders and
SMILE!

· O ·

A glad heart makes a happy face.
PROVERBS 15:13

Children will learn to speak
as they are spoken to.

· O ·

Do for others what you would like them to do for you.
MATTHEW 7:12

The time is now and the place is here.

· O ·

Today if you hear His voice, do not harden your hearts.
HEBREWS 3:7-8, NASB

When you're happy, I'm happy.
When you cry, I cry.

· O ·

When others are happy, be happy with them.
If they are sad, share their sorrow.
ROMANS 12:15

When you open your mouth,
your insides show.

· O ·

Whatever is in your heart determines what you say.
MATTHEW 12:34

Listen to your children;
you will learn something.

· O ·

A little child shall lead them.
ISAIAH 11:6, KJV

Mama Says...

Empty mothers speak empty words.
True wisdom comes from being
filled with God's Word.

· O ·

Let the word of Christ dwell in you richly.
COLOSSIANS 3:16, NIV

When we work together we get more
done and have twice the fun.

· O ·

Two people. . . get a better return for their labor.
ECCLESIASTES 4:9

Worry gives you wrinkles.

· O ·

Don't be troubled or afraid.
JOHN 14:27

Swimming equals a bath.

· O ·

Now we can really serve God, not in the old way by obeying
the letter of the law, but in the new way, by the Spirit.

ROMANS 7:6

Mama Says...

You are old when it takes longer
to rest than to get tired.

· O ·

And all the days of Methuselah were
nine hundred sixty and nine years.
GENESIS 5:27, KJV

From those to whom much is given,
much is expected.

· O ·

All must give as they are able, according to the blessings
given to them by the LORD your God.
DEUTERONOMY 16:16

Much is required from those to whom much is given,
and much more is required from those
to whom much more is given.
LUKE 12:48

Running off at the mouth runs people off.

· O ·

Being a fool makes you a blabbermouth.
ECCLESIASTES 5:3

Learn to laugh at yourself.

· O ·

Laughter can conceal a heavy heart.
PROVERBS 14:13

It's always darkest before dawn.

· O ·

The darkness is past, and the true light now shineth.

1 JOHN 2:8, KJV

It's easier for children to spend
your money than their money.

· O ·

Riches can disappear as though they had the wings of a bird!
PROVERBS 23:5

Mama Says...

He's just talking to hear himself talk.

· O ·

A fool's voice is known by multitude of words.
ECCLESIASTES 5:3, KJV

Don't brag about something before it happens.

· O ·

Don't brag about tomorrow,
since you don't know what the day will bring.
PROVERBS 27:1

You'll feel better tomorrow.

· O ·

I will not leave you comfortless: I will come to you.

JOHN 14:18, KJV

Where you're going is more important
than where you've been.

· O ·

Run, that ye may obtain.
1 CORINTHIANS 9:24, KJV

Mama Says...

Forgive and forget.

· O ·

You cannot stay angry with your people forever,
because you delight in showing mercy.

MICAH 7:18

Just do the best you can.

· O ·

I have fought a good fight,
I have finished my course,
I have kept the faith.
2 TIMOTHY 4:7, KJV

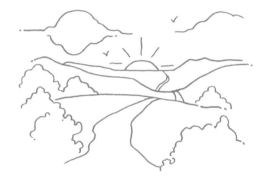

Your day will come.

· O ·

There is a time for everything,
a season for every activity under heaven.
ECCLESIASTES 3:1

Your life can change in an instant.

· O ·

We will all be transformed.
It will happen in a moment, in the blinking of an eye.
1 CORINTHIANS 15:51-52

Whatever you tell your child she cannot have
will be exactly what she wants the most.

· O ·

You want what you don't have, so you scheme.
JAMES 4:2

The best toys aren't always
the store-bought toys.

· O ·

Be satisfied with what you have.
HEBREWS 13:5

Mama Says...

Look for the face of Jesus in
the ones you care for.

· O ·

You took me in and cared for me
as though I were an angel from God,
or even Jesus Christ himself.
GALATIANS 4:14, TLB

The fault you see in your child is usually the fault you *don't* see in yourself.

· O ·

Stop judging others, and you will not be judged.
For others will treat you as you treat them.
Whatever measure you use in judging others,
it will be used to measure how you are judged.
MATTHEW 7:1-2

Mama Says...

Listening is learning.

· O ·

My dear brothers and sisters, be quick to listen, slow to
speak, and slow to get angry. Your anger can never make
things right in God's sight.

JAMES 1:19-20

The best thing we've got is each other.

· O ·

Listen to your father, who gave you life, and don't despise
your mother's experience when she is old.
PROVERBS 23:22

Children won't kill you,
but you'll never be the same.

· O ·

They are not the same anymore,
for the old life is gone. A new life has begun!
2 CORINTHIANS 5:17

Welcome to my help-yourself kitchen.

· O ·

Whoever does not work should not eat.
2 THESSALONIANS 3:10

If you're going to fight, go outside.

· O ·

Yanking a dog's ears is as foolish
as interfering in someone else's argument.
PROVERBS 26:17

If it were easy,
everybody'd
be doing it.

· O ·

Be strong and courageous, for your work will be rewarded.
2 CHRONICLES 15:7

Mama Says...

Be nice to your brother.

· O ·

How wonderful it is, how pleasant,
when brothers live together in harmony!
PSALM 133:1

Don't fan the flames.

· O ·

A hot-tempered person starts fights
and gets into all kinds of sin.
PROVERBS 29:22

Flowers have faces.

· O ·

Young woman:
"I am the rose of Sharon, the lily of the valley."
SONG OF SONGS 2:1

Coming home should be fun.

· O ·

A dry crust eaten in peace
is better than a great feast with strife.
PROVERBS 17:1

Be a willing back scratcher,
for as long as possible.

· O ·

The smell of my son is the good smell
of the open fields that the LORD has blessed.
GENESIS 27:27

Food tastes better on a pretty plate.

· O ·

Go ahead. Eat your food and drink your wine
with a happy heart, for God approves of this!
ECCLESIASTES 9:7

Mama Says...

When you see the baby,
you'll forget all about the labor.

· O ·

When her child is born, her anguish gives place to joy
because she has brought a new person into the world.

JOHN 16:21

Birthdays are the best days of the year.

· O ·

Suddenly, the angel was joined by a vast host of
others—the armies of heaven—praising God:
"Glory to God in the highest heaven,
and peace on earth to all whom God favors."
LUKE 2:13-14

I love fat-legged babies.

· O ·

His legs are as pillars of marble,
set upon sockets of fine gold.
SONG OF SOLOMON 5:15, KJV

Children's art is fabulous! Frame it.

When I was a child, I spoke and
thought and reasoned as a child does.
1 CORINTHIANS 13:11

When you feel a bee in your hair,
let somebody else get it out.

· O ·

Better is a neighbour that is near than a brother far off.
PROVERBS 27:10, KJV

You can't get the toothpaste back in the tube.

· O ·

Keep away from every kind of evil.
1 THESSALONIANS 5:22

Don't be a busybody.

· O ·

This should be your ambition: to live a quiet life,
minding your own business and working with your hands.
1 THESSALONIANS 4:11

Blow a kiss to your grandmother.

· O ·

Grandchildren are the crowning glory of the aged.
PROVERBS 17:6

Mama Says...

When you make a cake, be sure there's
plenty left in the mixing bowl to lick.

· O ·

My cup overflows with blessings.

PSALM 23:5

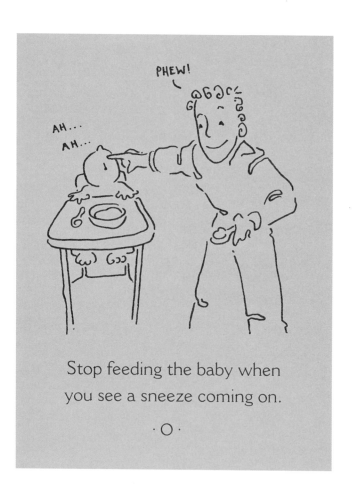

Stop feeding the baby when
you see a sneeze coming on.

· O ·

Hold thou me up, and I shall be safe.
PSALM 119:117, KJV

Mama Says...

Walk barefoot on rocks with your children.

· O ·

Share each other's troubles and problems.
GALATIANS 6:2

Read the same book over
and over if you're asked.

· O ·

Repeat them again and again to your children.
DEUTERONOMY 6:7

Mama Says...

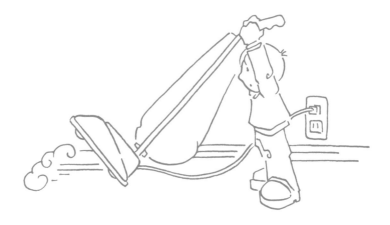

Hard work never hurt anybody.

· O ·

Do you see any truly competent workers?
They will serve kings rather than ordinary people.

PROVERBS 22:29

The same answer heard twice—once from
Mom and once from Dad—is twice as strong.

· O ·

Two people can accomplish more than twice as much as one.
ECCLESIASTES 4:9

Mama Says...

Teach your child how to live
with life's burdens rather than
how to escape from them.

· O ·

The LORD is good. When trouble comes, he is a strong refuge.
And he knows everyone who trusts in him.

NAHUM 1:7

Smile and your child will smile back.

· O ·

As in water face reflects face,
so the heart of man reflects man.
PROVERBS 27:19, NASB

Success breeds success.

· O ·

They go from strength to strength.
PSALM 84:7, KJV

Someone needs these words today.
Someone needs these words.
Take my hand and write through me,
Tell me what to say.

· O ·

Timely advice is as lovely as golden apples in a silver basket.
PROVERBS 25:11

The best book you'll ever read will be the one you write yourself. Now it's your turn. What you have to say to your child is really what's important. The real value of this "Mama Says" book is to stimulate your own thinking. And the notes you've made in this book could be the beginning of a new method of communicating with your child. Every moment you spend in reading, writing, or researching with your child as the focus of your attention will be time well spent. You'll have two gifts: a tangible book and the opportunity to become a new and better mother as you develop your own relationship with God through listening and discernment as God speaks to you. What more could a child ask for?

Here is my recipe for writing a "Mama Says" book. You will develop and refine your own method, but for now, these are my suggestions on how to begin.

One more thing: don't be offended if your handiwork is not read immediately. Someday, when the child is ready, he or she will appreciate your efforts. For today, be satisfied with your own best effort, and remember . . .

"Tell your children what they need to hear. That's the best you can do."

Train up a child in the way he should go:
and when he is old, he will not depart from it.
PROVERBS 22:6, KJV

Materials

- Inspirational reading material
- Pencil and paper (a junior legal pad is my favorite)
- Blank book (I like a spiral-bound book so I can make changes easily.)
- Resource books
- Computer (optional) to input your material—but when I'm reading, I use a pencil and paper to take notes.

Method

- Find a time and place conducive to reading and writing—this is the hardest part.
- Read until you're ready to write. God will speak to you as you read.
- Jot down thoughts and reflections while reading or whenever you remember things your mother, grandmother, aunt, and mentors said.
- Free-associate. You can organize your scribbles later.
- Keep your notes. You may want to develop a filing system or computer program for this information.
- Transfer (rewrite) your notes into a blank book. Personalize with photos, stencils, cutouts, drawings—anything that makes an inviting book for your child.
- Use a topical resource book for help with Scripture references and a quotation resource book for famous quotations.

- Give each page a theme (or subject).
- Give yourself plenty of time. For example, set a goal of one year or for a graduation, wedding, birthday, or Christmas gift. This is an ongoing project, so revel in the process.
- Enjoy your time alone with God as you partner in communication with your child. Mother Teresa said, "I am just a little pencil, the work is God's work" (*A Gift for God*).

Favorite Resource Books

- *The Complete Book of Bible Quotations*
- *The Handbook of Bible Application*
- *The New Strong's Exhaustive Concordance*
- *Today's Parallel Bible*; New International Version, Updated Edition; *New American Standard Bible*; King James Version; New Living Translation
- *The TouchPoint Bible*
- Feel free to use any quotations from this book!

Favorite Inspirational Reading

- *Adventure in Prayer*, Catherine Marshall
- *Becoming a Woman of Influence*, Carol Kent
- *Beyond Ourselves*, Catherine Marshall
- *The Burden Is Light*, Eugenia Price
- *A Closer Walk*, Catherine Marshall
- *Disciplines of a Beautiful Woman*, Anne Ortland
- *The Friendship Factor*, Alan Loy McGinnis
- *The Fruit of the Spirit*, Sarah Hornsby

- *A Gift for God*, Mother Teresa
- *The Helper*, Catherine Marshall
- *How to Keep a Spiritual Journal*, Ronald Klug
- *Lord, Change Me*, Evelyn Christenson
- *Make Love Your Aim*, Eugenia Price
- *Mr. Jones, Meet the Master*, Catherine Marshall
- *Speak Up with Confidence*, Carol Kent
- *Something Beautiful for God*, Malcolm Muggeridge
- *Soul Feast*, Marjorie Thompson
- *Walking on Water*, Madeleine L'Engle
- *Woman to Woman*, Eugenia Price

For information on scheduling Rita Maggart to speak for your event, please contact Speak Up Speaker Services toll free at (888) 870-7719 or email: speakupinc@aol.com

Mama Says...

Mama Says...

Mama Says...

Mama Says...

Mama Says...

Mama Says . . . You Can Always
  Come Home for Advice
Kitchen table wisdom from the heart

Mama Says . . . Don't Drive Faster
  Than Your Guardian Angel Can Fly
A care package from home

Mama Says . . . Cookies Cure a
  Lot of Things
Encouragement for new parents